Some Days
the Spoons Talk Back

Some Days the Spoons Talk Back

Poems by

Chuck Madansky

© 2021 Chuck Madansky. All rights reserved.
This material may not be reproduced in any form, published,
reprinted, recorded, performed, broadcast,
rewritten or redistributed without
the explicit permission of Chuck Madansky.
All such actions are strictly prohibited by law.

Cover design by Shay Culligan

Cover Art by Cindy Wood
Painted on vintage book pages in oil and watercolor,
this painting was inspired by
the poetry in this book

ISBN: 978-1-63980-030-8

Kelsay Books
502 South 1040 East, A-119
American Fork, Utah 84003
Kelsaybooks.com

To Wilderness
the best part of everything

Acknowledgments

Grateful acknowledgment is given to the following journals and anthologies where poems in this book have previously appeared, often in different versions or with different titles:

Truth Serum Press: "Duende"
Cape Cod Poetry Review: "The Blindfold's Eyes"
Pure Slush: "A Different Kind of Light"
Muddy River Poetry Review: "A Question of Winter," "The Golden Rule"
Wising Up Press: "What We Feed the Earth"
Outrider Press: "On Finding a Dead Loon at Crosby Beach"
Passager: "The Difference Between One Day and the Next Is Whether the Spoons Talk Back," "We Didn't Think of Death"
WCAI Radio: "Only Long," "Edge," "Saint Francis and the Birds," "A Different Kind of Light," "The Indifference of Nature"
Brewster Ladies Library: "Tethered," "This Is What Democracy Looks Like", "By Hook or By Crook"
Cape Cod Times: "We Knew"
First Parish Press: "When Push Comes to Shove"
Cape Healing Arts Magazine: "The Story Isn't Over Yet"
Seabird Music: "The Old Country"
Nightingale & Sparrow: "The Dappled Forest"

"The Wave" was a Finalist in the Cultural Center of Cape Cod 2015 Poetry Competition.

"The Difference Between One Day and the Next is Whether the Spoons Talk Back" won Honorable Mention in the Passager Poetry Contest 2019.

"Ailanthus" won First Honorable Mention in the annual Joe Gouveia WOMR Poetry Competition 2019, judged by Marge Piercy.

With great gratitude:

to my editors at Kelsay Books, Karen Kelsay, Delisa Hargrove and Shay Culligan for their excellence, support and encouragement;

to Cindy Wood for her generous heart and the gift of her artwork on the cover;

to my teachers for their gifts of skill and spirit: Galway Kinnell, Marie Howe, Carolyn Forche´, Dorianne Laux, Marilyn Nelson, John Murillo, Frank Gaspar, Mark Doty, Martha Collins, Lorna Blake, Nickole Brown, Jessica Jacobs, Ada Limon, Kevin Young, Cyrus Cassells, Matthew Olzmann, and Kim Addonizio;

to my poetry colleagues for their support and feedback over the years: Janine Certo, James Wyshynski, Leo Thibault, Donna O'Connell, Dianne Ashley, Margaret Phillips, Margaret Rice Moir, Susan Graesser, Ginia Pati, Lucile Burt, Paula Erickson, Marjorie Block, deer Sullivan, Diane Pansire, Twinks Hastings, Alyson Adler and Wilderness Sarchild;

to Alyson Adler and Jessica Jacobs for their in-depth reading and invaluable assistance in ordering and revising this manuscript;

and to my wife, the poet and playwright Wilderness Sarchild, without whose love and encouragement this work could never have come to fruition.

Contents

I.

Once More the Round	15
I Eat an Apple and Wonder if This Is What Rilke Meant	16
This Unexpected Grace	18
A Different Kind of Light	19
Last night's rain	20
Ailanthus	21
The Dappled Forest	22
A Question of Winter	23
Edge	24
The Prayer I Could Not Utter	25
The Innkeeper's Song	26

II.

High Stakes	29
We Knew	30
Number the Stars	31
The Blindfold's Eyes	32
The Old Country	33
Israel/Palestine	34
Conviction	35
as an example	36
Absolution with a Twist	37
Pickup Games	38
Ode to P.O. Box 2034, Brewster, MA	39
What We Feed the Earth	40
Home is Where	41

III.

The Difference Between One Day and the Next Is	
Whether the Spoons Talk Back	45
My Father Comes Back as a Blue Jay	46
Couches	47
What a Jar Can Hold	48
The Weight We Carry	49
Adoption	50
The Story I Tell Myself	51
Inside/Out	52
Crabs	54
Isaac, Years Later in Therapy	55
The Real Prayer	56

IV.

St. Francis and the Birds	59
The Indifference of Nature	60
Birefringence	61
As Above, So Below	62
What Fills the Silence	63
Duende	64
Only Long	65
Frayed Music	66
Elegy	67
Thou, Nature	68
I asked the insects	69

V.

I Was Without a World	73
step-love	74
One Good Turn	75
Tethered	76
What Words Miss	77
Things to Think	78
We Didn't Think of Death	79
When I say I fell in love	80
Anniversary	81
The Wave	82
There Is Nothing but Space Between Us	83
Inis Mor	84
Tashlik	85

I.

Once More the Round

I'll tell you right off—the house is the self—
and we built the house too small. Sure,
we need jobs and people to love us, but we,
full of ourselves and windowless, only
saw what we were missing when grace
and tragedy punched peepholes through
and all we could do was watch
as the gods wrestled our squirming souls
from out the muck of the world.
So death left us behind until we became
nothing but photographs left in a drawer,
names and dates in faded ink.
When the kids of the kids of the kids
tossed us finally we were free

and followed our bodies through dissolution
to simple compounds, the food of roots,
promoted to sweet black tupelo fruit,
fed to a chickadee, downsized to eggshell,
on to a life as a blueberry bush, browsed
by a deer for a short career as antler velvet,
scraped into soil then swayed as sedges a season or two.
Grass seed to mouse ear to mouse ear chickweed,
compost, tomato and thieving crow,
always remembering, never forgetting
to leave a door open, to keep our souls close.

And then becoming human again, tragic
and amnesiac, building the house too small.

I Eat an Apple and Wonder if This Is What Rilke Meant

You must change your life.
                    —*Rilke*

Delicious, this becoming
each other can go on and on,

is and is not the end of you—
the orchard rain, bees'

sex, now in the field
of our affection—I not I

but us, fog of cider,
cry of split wood

as your body succumbs,
the mottled blush of you,

shreds in my mouth, a dance
we already knew, chewing

into your notion of sweetness,
mine of learning tongues,

yours of roots and loss,
mine of meeting hunger.

Unlike Jonah, swallowed,
you don't reappear,

but we watch together
the ochre come over

your flesh exposed, the ragged
rhyme of tooth and life

unflowered, a rain-forced
roseblood, starburst flush,

a way for us to be
more things at once.

I wanted to devour you
but only for this:

between branch and earth,
now we fall together.

This Unexpected Grace

The face of our love has begun to wrinkle.
Lines emerge around the eyes and mouth.
It is not just we who laugh

and squint and weep, but this love
which laughs at us as well, knowing more than we
of what is to come and beyond.

Neither of us ever expected this grace.
The inroads and rooting of love itself
has made us who we are.

The face of our love laughs
at our squabbles, our fears, our doubts.
The soil of us darkens; the rain of us quickens.

Husband and wife,
we melt in time
to the life beneath life.

A Different Kind of Light

When I've eaten all the chips,
I write it on the list,
and soon there will be more.
This more has followed me from birth.
The earth has tilted just so,
has shaken the not-so-much,
the less, the never, onto other lives,
other lists. I have visited
their houses and bare shelves,
their cardboard on the street grates,
and handed "some" to them,
knowing there was always more.

O, the secret price of more—
blankets laced with smallpox,
produce picked for pennies,
blue jeans sewn in chains.

Torches lead the way
to keep the world
on tilt to more…
we need a different
kind of light
to say *Enough.*

Last night's rain

sits like a pox, yellow and even-beaded
on the slick green silken back of the water shield

floating in placid herds on the pond
which bears itself and the memory of ice and is held in turn

by sand and wood and the dense salt sea
and under that the Canadian Shield and under that

the metallic core which tumbles but will not yield.
It is a question—how much each of us can bear

and willingly suffer and not do our neighbors in. The sun
comes out and now the leaves bear topaz laced with amber.

Ailanthus

Years before the final break
I lost my friend.

He was visiting the Cape
and as we drove down Tubman Road

he pointed to some trees
and said, *I like their shape.*

How easy it would have been
to look and love them too—

I do now—but instead I said
Oh those, they're only sumacs.

An ignorant thing to say—
only.

They were actually Trees of Heaven,
redeeming our cities

one polluted block at a time.
Like a fool, I parroted

my girlfriend at the time
who disdained the common

and me. My friend said nothing
but I knew—years later

when he turned his back on me
for a trifle—why he left:

what was beautiful to him
had meant nothing to me.

The Dappled Forest

In the old stories, one tree looks just like another
and soon, you are hopelessly lost.

You come to a clearing—a cottage—and your panic melts.
You just feel sheepish, relieved.

Smoke, the sweet smell of barbeque, pours from the roof—
maybe they'll ask you to lunch. The knocker crumbles like sugar.

Naive to think that things are better, just because
we can see the sun. The old ones knew about shadows,

how night is the shadow of Earth, and the absence of light
is the least of what blooms at dusk.

The forest reveals itself in moist fragrance, quiet tones of rust
and green, in stillness the brilliance of daylight dissolves.

Turn and re-enter the uncertain light.

A Question of Winter

In a toe-numb
bone-ache winter,
the hellebore
opens its snow-
white blossom,
as if to say
you, too, could
do this, only see
how one thing stands
behind the next,
pulling the circle
of time, how for
and against
are broken
in seamlessness.

You and I
are frozen
before the flower.
Ice heaves
on the pond.
A great horned owl
flutes a question
into the silence:
Whose side
are you on?

We rise
from the ground,
mittens knitted together.
Which side
of spring
is winter on?
I could never
leave you.

Edge

When I saw you on the edge,
I had to think of you falling.
The wind, only lately beloved,
was fierce against the cliffs.

And I wondered would I
follow you in, not to save
what couldn't be saved, but
only because you are my edge,

nothing before or after.

The Prayer I Could Not Utter

Afraid of death, I made a kind of death
of life—I'd tear at the walls and infold—
while glib philosophies all weighed less
than a suffering world too weighted to hold.
Languishing under a cynical spell,
a bitter pill to keep me from waking,
unable to pray, like a dumbstruck bell
withholding its song from over-shaking,

I cracked at last, unshelled by grief to grieve,
shucked by pain to feel, freed to surrender,
a man turned inside out to receive
the gift of a riven heart made tender:
The prayer I could not utter came to be
the one that brought me down to bended knee.

The Innkeeper's Song

Before they knocked, the house knew
and unlocked the door.

The brick walkway supported their steps,
the windows breathed in time with their breath.

Tired, hungry, scared, lost—the last ones you might trust
with your mother's vase or the good silver—I turned them away.

The walls sighed, the roof hung its head in shame,
they already knew what gives us birth,

how wise people follow the stars,
and even the straw on the barn floor is lighted.

If only I had let them in, my lonely manger might shine from afar,
and my house would hold me again.

II.

High Stakes

This is how he grows: by being defeated...
                                      —Rilke

The angel's office is in a mall, a storefront featuring **God is Love**
t-shirts and bumper stickers—she's a low-level seraph, stuck
with marginal cases. We agree to a game of cards—
less sweaty than wrestling.

The angel sits across from me and plays her first card—
the rippled arms of a tupelo. I trump with burnt koalas.
She comes back strong with a child's laughter,
I tender an infant caged at the border.
Angel: *The arm-around-you smell of a dog,*
Me: *The alcohol swab before the vet's needle.*
She slaps down dawn,
I counter with cancer.

On we grapple, the stars disappear.
Undone, bone-tired, I play my last card—grief.
The angel touches the hollow
of my hip. I forget my name.
The margins of her head are backlit
by willows.

We Knew

And when the last giraffe is gone from the earth—
that absurd bowing and kneeling to lap a drink
with pink and purple tongue—
and acacias, accustomed to being browsed,
become accustomed to loss,

when nothing with a neck longer than an ostrich,
nothing with horns like gear shifts, nothing
that stands still as death at sunset
and lopes with the grace of a slow-moving wave
is left except as an image, a story, a meal

remembered, and children ask
how could it happen, do not pretend
we didn't know, don't cavil and stammer
absurd excuses—accustom yourself
to answer: *it was a slow-moving death—*

we wouldn't stop, even to grieve.

Number the Stars

My father's people were called *Melamed,*
the ones in the *shtetl* too silly to do much
but teach the children their ABC's.
Silly used to mean *blessed* or *happy.*
Perfectly silly to have taken the children
to the forest to learn to speak bird,
silly to have kept them there,
having heard shots scythe the village,
silly to play *quiet-as-a-star-hiding-in-the-sky,*
to have taken them underwing after.
This instinct to keep the children alive,
to save them for the grief ahead, and the time
when grief becomes something else.

The Blindfold's Eyes

for Dianna Ortiz, an American nun, kidnapped and tortured by the Guatemalan military in 1989, under the auspices of the CIA.

Scarred back:
sacred tobacco
burnt on a nun
for the wrong gods.

How to make a machete
kill: Take a nun
31 years old
and hold her hands
on the handle...
The blindfold sees
what can't be told.

The stones are just
beginning to speak
the last sounds
of the first ones
to die in the hole
in the cellar.

White House counsel
Alberto Gonzales
swallows the cool
artesian water,
dries his hands
with a folded napkin,
takes a drag
on his cigarette
and calls the meeting
to order.

The Old Country

Brussels is all sunlit farmland,
but the first voice I hear in German
frightens me.

Then Poland is dark clouds
and smokestacks, green and lush.

There, behind those trees,
we could hide.

Spirits, in the old country,
showing me the ropes.

Israel/Palestine

Rain, soil, warmth and wind
create a human being.

Salt and water
from acid and lye.

Steel
from iron and coal.

Razor wire
cuts both ways.

Conviction

If a whale swallowed me whole
or a saint healed my wounds

would you believe it?
Would you doubt it if I said

I saved a lion from a thorn?
Already my grandkids insist

trees don't talk, stones don't sing,
frogs should never be kissed.

If I flew for you now,
would I deserve your faith?

If I made it rain in Gaza
would the occupation end?

Would immigrants be welcome
if I disappeared the walls?

Shall I turn water into wine,
or will they kill me?

as an example

[[88 are penned]]
[[standing room only]]
[[weeks on the border]]
[[think tender veal]]
[[or Auschwitz]]
[[where pens]]
[[held them to stand]]
[[until they died]]
[[torture]]
[[has many hands]]
[[kids]]
[[in the hands of men]]
[[in a room]]
[[with no room]]
[[the last word]]
[[to be penned]]
[[is tender]]

Absolution with a Twist

The knife is innocent with its razor
blade. The grass is innocent growing by
blood. The heart, innocent in its pleasure,
beating. Likewise, the eye behind the eye,
seeing. Subtract all the innocence from
all that is. Then notice who's ripe to blame.
The all-that's-left thinks it's such a shame,
til it sees itself, and recounts the sum.
We're innocently caught, between our selves
and holy nature. Nature never delves
beyond itself, absolute and given.
But poor, blameful self is ever driven
to seek absolution fraught with a twist:
to solve the problem, it cannot exist.

Pickup Games

I pulled into the local P.O. The very last spot
was slender. The guy the next car
over took issue and grabbed me, his hot

breath in my face, and threw me hard
against the cab of my truck.
I mention my truck because I was on guard

when a man came into the local cafe, looked
at me, asked if that pickup outside
was mine. Then he reached out and shook

my hand. My bumper sticker and he agreed.
And that makes me wonder if the Navy guy
who backed into me actually did see

my truck, contrary to what he said. My
bumper sticker—End Torture Now—
follows me gamely wherever I go.

Ode to P.O. Box 2034, Brewster, MA

This is how I know
we're friends:
Even when you're empty,
you don't change
the lock.
You stay the perfect
height for me
to bow and plumb
your inwardness,
a shaman's hole,
a tunnel to enveloped things.
Hope chest,
debt coffer,
little man's sarcophagus
unburied with my dead
mother's mail.
Case hardened
junk dealer,
treasured vault
of tongues,
you're a steady date,
the back door
to a wailing wall.
You hold me blameless
when I leave you,
give me all
within your walls
and the everything
outside them
they imply.
.

What We Feed the Earth

Why did I ask to meet him at the coffee shop?
I didn't want him to know where I lived.

His letters to the editor on immigration were filled with pain
and enough self-righteousness to match my own letters back.

I made the invitation. He agreed to meet, and we met.
We lived in the same town, were about the same age,

found enough to laugh at together. When I asked why
he felt so strongly about ending immigration

he said something about not wanting to *lose our way of life,*
which I took to mean white, and in control.

Later, I learned something else beneath the pain:
his brother had died of an overdose, and he blamed

that death on the drugs, and the drugs on immigration.
The last time I wrote, I said I was sorry to learn of his loss.

Why haven't we ever met again? I don't know how to meet
his grief. If the earth isn't fed with tears, we feed it with blood.

Home is Where

The tupelo is an American tree,
its arms, from the heartwood, open.
Likewise, the chestnut—breadbasket, blighted.
Pitch pine, tough as an immigrant,
goes through fire to come to life.
A forest can begin again
from just an inch of willow.
Sycamore, tamarack, oak and spruce
belong wherever they grow.
The American tree
is whatever grows in America.

III.

The Difference Between One Day and the Next Is Whether the Spoons Talk Back

What does it mean
that I talk to the dishes,
to the bowls and spoons as I wash them,
the philodendron over the sink
I greet and assess for thirst,
the tourmaline by my bed,
the hat I wear to sleep,
the boots that slip on so easily?

I think I know why my mom
only cried when she drank
at family parties, the grief
built up from days alone
with her battered aluminum pan,
potatoes cut and waiting to boil,
the house quiet and empty,
blessedly alone and lonely,
free, but freed from her dreams.

There are times I don't want
to be touched at all
and others, if not for clothes
and blankets and wind,
I'd die of loneliness.
I know this, know it so well
I could shake it like salt
over mashed potatoes
and you could taste my life.

My Father Comes Back as a Blue Jay

With raucous abandon
he calls me outside, he
who was always so muted
and calm, reasoned, secular
hopping from branch
to branch, showing off
his wings, the glint of his talons.
He scatters the seed
I lay out for him, screaming
*hurry up and grow
a pair—fly with me!*
He's so surprised
that there was more.

Couches

Mother is in her place on the beige couch,
drink held fast against her trembling knees,
the ice succumbing, the knife already comfortable
amid its cousins on the table,
little pan of potatoes set to boil
on my father's return. Mother tries
to remember what the doctor said.
What do I have to be angry at?

She looks to the back-porch door,
locked. She would never return
to that doctor's couch, the radium
of her dreams would never grow dim,
she held on to our arms and shopping
carts for years until whatever it was
had passed.

My sister and I recite lines
from the plays mother never
acted in. Neither of us had
biological children. I think of her
each afternoon when I drink.
I still love mashed potatoes.

What a Jar Can Hold

I've been seeing beetles lately.
Big and small—scary ones that only
emerge from their underground roost
to lay their eggs on my stairway;
junebugs, loitered into July,
who don't like letting go, even in death.

The little ones, metallic, remind me
of grabbing handfuls when I was ten
from the roses they loved to snuffle and chew.
Mr. Ingber would pay us a dime
for a pint jar full of their copper
and opaline green. Packed
and freighted for death, they smelled
the way that people smell when they begin to cry—
rain on hot pavement—ozone, rot.

I was old enough to know
what Mr. Ingber would do with that jar.
I should have let them go.
And now I open that jar, in me,
gasoline evaporated, beetle bodies dust,
my small repentance, late.

Maybe love is never lost.
If so, it might collect somewhere:
Mr. Ingber's love of roses,
my love for the beetles here,
all packed inside an empty jar,
waiting to be opened.

The Weight We Carry

Once, in little league, I tried to stretch a triple into a home run.
The umpire called me out.

I argued, and the catcher sat on my head.
People laughed. In the dark furrow of his ass,

I couldn't breathe. I still can't
wear shirts or sweaters that touch my neck.

The simple truth of breath when you can't breathe,
standing when you're crushed,

finding a way to bear the weight we carry.

Adoption

You chose me
and brought me
to the golden door
of your family,
but part of me
never walked through.

I steal your stuff
and go through your closet
when you're not home.
Call it a womb
and you'll understand.

I want what lies
next to your skin
and shadows your eyes
when you look at me.
I want the smell and taste of you,
I want to walk inside your shoes
as if they were my own.

You don't want me
to take your things,
but I'm not after what isn't mine.
I'm looking for my innocence.

If I could open the closet inside you
and rub against the soft dark shapes.
If it were me to perfume your days,
and me who you saw
in the make-up mirror,
I would not need to be a thief,
but the daughter and heir of the golden door,
and I would know you cherished me
and we would be a family.

The Story I Tell Myself

Once upon a time I was left alone
for several nights in the hospital.
No one living knows why this was done
to a newborn. The moon spoke a riddle

for several nights in the hospital,
replacing abandonment with light.
To a newborn the moon spoke a riddle:
Where is your mother, unless you're my sun,

replacing abandonment with light?
The moon caressed and bathed me in the night.
Where is your mother unless you're my sun?
My mother has left now and doesn't return.

The moon caressed and bathed me in the night.
No one living knows why this was done.
My mother has left now and doesn't return.
Once upon a time I was left alone.

Inside/Out

1. There are two sides to a page, though the ink on the other side often shows through, like looking into water, or windows, or eyes. And what of death, of which there is so much to feel, and so little to say, the water itself my father's last breath, the tear that slipped from his eye? Isn't it all revealed on the surface, hidden in the shape of the world, one side to everything?

2. I call it calling one heart to another, when love for the songs of crickets and katydids leads me to seek out their stories and forms, and then they appear on my car, or my windows and screens. Or I pray to the spirit of milkweed to help give a friend just a taste of death, then milkweed begins to grow through my walkway. Something there is that wants to be known, that migrates into the field of affection, as if there were more light to live and grow by there.

3. Everything with a name is misnamed. Ordinary words are anything but. Pond, ripple, shimmer: if these were only what they seem, then why should they sparkle less when men refuse to shed their tears of grief? The chair, the floor, the earth that holds you also repels you. The green of trees is what trees reject. Something is being told through the world, and what it seems like it isn't. Except that it is.

4. And now, a setting off, which is breath released and ripples played on a pond. A never-to-return which turns us back toward immensity, to scratch at the bark, play hide and seek, a turtle that peeks its head above water and, mostly afraid, swims under again. Are we annuals or perennials? Hawk and osprey, birds of prayer, you need sharp talons to prise the layers of name and word, habit and fear, to what lies beneath the verb to be.

5. Boluses of blue and gray—fabric of silk that the wind makes painted, wrinkled—the surface is enough to love.

6. The heart that makes us human makes us afraid. Light pours through a broken heart, from the outside in and the inside out.

Crabs

for my parents

We crack claws, pull belly keys,
expose mustard guts,
settle to the serious work
of picking meat from corpses,
dirty-handed with spices,
a mile, just, from where
we circled your graves
with chocolate and wine.

Now the little legs,
the steamed heap,
the neap tide pitcher of beer
disappear into us
as surely as did you.

I won't come back
to not find you anymore.

But to the crabs—
the way the large hard
protect the soft small,
the wisdom of leaving
a shell to grow—

And to the Chesapeake,
Blue Point oysters,
fine mud, the familiar sun,
the stars.

Isaac, Years Later in Therapy

...Then Avram reached out his hand and took the knife to his son.
—Genesis 22:1-19

This was after my father got
Hagar the maidservant pregnant
and sent her away with my brother.
All the times he raped her
before she conceived, or promised
they'd run off together, after. Liar.

He beat my mother Sarah up and down
the wood branch hovel of our home,
swearing she was a whore, on and on,
And then he'd turn to me and smile
that dead-eyed grimace—*You're next.*

So, as usual, off we go to make
blah blah blah to his god. And he
cold-cocks me soon as we get up the hill.
Strips me, binds me, the lichen crust
on the altar grinds my back.
He's mumbling to voices in his head,
a kind of froth stuck between his lips.
He lifts his knife

and a ram comes out of nowhere
(believe me, this place was a desert)
and butts Avram's ass—he lurches and sinks
the knife in the ram, screaming, again
and again. Later, after he slit the throat
and drank the blood, he looks at me
and shakes his head. Without a word,
he cuts me free.

When she heard what he did,
my mother died of grief.

The Real Prayer

When I need to die
to my smaller self, I close
my eyes and tell my mind to say *Lord,
make me an instrument of Thy peace,*
without lapsing into memories
of the *piano* my mother played until
she got nervous, or the *piece* of cheesecake
left in the fridge—and after maybe twenty
minutes, the silence between the words
starts to thicken,

and the one who needs and prays recedes
and the one who sees and hears is there
and the real prayer, which never stops,
begins.

IV.

St. Francis and the Birds

Maybe they got the story wrong.
I think St. Francis went to the woods,
the way we go to the Beech Forest now,
and stood among the pines, while larks
ate breadcrumbs from his hands.

Maybe the larks felt at ease with him
and stayed while he croaked
in a broken voice
all the questions that clawed at his heart:

Why are there lepers, why are there poor,
why so much shame, and don't You care?
Why are there so many unanswered prayers?

The birds were patient.
They let him finish.
Waited for the noise to end.
They hopped and shifted on his arms.

He noticed that they were there—
the weight of them,
their little claws, their perfect eyes,
their song began.

It was the birds who preached to him,
who lifted light into the air,
who told the truth, and with no shame,
left Francis as if born again.

The Indifference of Nature

for Natasha Trethewey

It is true that a virus is killing us.
That virus loves the fat of our cells,
the glistening of our inner nose and throat,
the wet forest maze of our lungs,
and is loved by our cells, who give it everything,
hold nothing back, and all of this is nature.
And when we breathe in, inspired to feel
the quelling of desire again, and then
let it out to get back to what we once felt,
it is our nature to do so, to love
the exhalation as much as the taking in.
And when we can't breathe easy any more,
when our lungs have turned to ground glass
and we realize that death—which we loved
to deny, despite its steadfast patience
and hunger for us—that death has readied
its arms to disarm us at last, into whatever
awaits beyond the love we knew
when we were human and in love,
and not indifferent, then the love beyond
love will take us, naturally, and the light
within us, and go on and on, lighted.

Birefringence

I write for the dark times,
when the two kinds of light

lie *normal* to each other,
where all the angles are right

and only the blur of seeing double,
the rhombohedron of paradox,

can light the way—thanks to those
who hold the unity of light, who bend it

and we call bent, who Gandhi-like,
see friend in enemy, joy in suffering,

freedom in resistance
by a crystal-clear heart.

In times of peace, we hold
the crystal just so, and go about

our human way—gardening,
thinking what we already know,

blind to what sees through us,
kind until we're not.

As Above, So Below

It's a mess down here,
leaf litter of strip mall
cousins going at it
all wrong, a brindled
presence, dimmed
undimmable, flickering
neon war—too few giraffes,
too many people, pinata'd
by time—a rainbow
of salt marsh and bloody noses,
gladiators and gladiolas,
tourmaline and torture.

O heart,

little sack of iron ore,
chafing dish for tears,
master of mosaic,
how to bear, let pass,
assent? Here, my squishy
tick-tock, is a tide creek
to write on—the problem
with the problem is the problem—
no up or down,
against or for,
nowhere to ascend—
only one game, one love:
as below, so above.

What Fills the Silence

The silence of frogs is more terrible
than when I say something cruel that I know
I'll need to make amends for, and babble
on instead. And maybe they didn't go

extinct, maybe they're just late this year—
denial is a hopeful kind of fear.
No plunks or harrumphs, no mating toad's scream,
but a pond of absence, a dearth of din.

The frogs knew how to live within two spheres;
our losses leave us stranded in but one.
It's loneliness we wanted to be done—
instead, our desperation built us biers.

What fills the silence we can't even see.
Who gave us frogs now gives us memories.

Duende

That wound, a light
white binding, pointing
slightly heartward
on the first finger
from my right thumb,
the one that flicks
gypsy moth worms
from my left forearm
in this season
of green devouring.

My mother
told me not to ride
my bike so fast
and I did and clipped
my finger on the left
fin of a Chevy Impala,
chrome bloodied—
the slight smile
on my mother's mouth.

Only Long

> *If there is a real desire, if the thing desired is really light, the desire for light produces it.*
> —Simone Weil

We long for help and the angels awaken.
But before the fragrance of our longing
can reach their nostrils, we close the bottle.
They were just brushing their teeth.
Before the music of our need can reach their ears,
we pawn our violins. Before the fruits of our desire
can ripen, we sell the orchard. To the Friend,
this longing smells like baking bread.
Angels gather in unruly crowds
to hear the music that reminds them
of why they have wings. What we call help
feeds on what we want to end.
Have compassion. They haven't had their breakfast yet.
Wells will dig themselves, if only we thirst,
deep and long.

Frayed Music

Each morning, a ruby throated hummingbird
plucks the old strings of a spider's web
and carries the frayed music back to her nest.

She makes her bed, smoothing the notes
into cracks that have opened in her dreams.

By noon she is ready to drink and fight.
The old tunes stick in her head like a bone.
By dusk she is worn to a frazzle.

She dreams of the raveled velvet cup she grew up in,
the purring to and fro of her mother's wings.

The feathered sheets are a mess. Once the sun stops staring,
she slips into the air that won't stop touching.

Elegy

There will be asters this autumn,
as if the sky had fallen,
as if the stars felt bereft
and enfolded to the Earth—

now in its fever throes,
oil-sick, lie-weary, burnt out
from men who act like boys—

asters will grow as never before,
will carpet the over-watered soil,
will ornament the coffin lids
where flowers fall like stars.

Thou, Nature

Nature's an *it*, the world goes on saying,
a thing undeserving of *he* or *she*,
relations so poor, they merit weighing
and selling but not an eternity.
Though weaver-birds weave and elephants weep
and trees warn each other of coming loss;
though dolphins outsmart us and fleas outleap
us, we go on constructing Nature's cross.
Attention to all the ways of being
alive might bring us alive a new way,
addressing Nature as Thou, and freeing
our words and our hearts to mean what they say.
Perhaps in Nature's ways we'd see the proof,
if only we could learn to speak the truth.

I asked the insects

what they were singing.
They said *our wings
were made for song—
we fly because we sing.
What brings us to heaven
is praise.*

V.

I Was Without a World

In my dream I was touching
your naked hip—
the little scars and stretch marks.
And I couldn't believe
we wouldn't always
be together, that Death
would have to pull us apart.

In the dream, Death was a woman.
I was without a world.
Then I woke to you
padding by to pee,
nightgown billowing silk.
I can't believe my luck.
I list the world, and first is you.

step-love

this is my step-world—i did not create it.
these are my step-trees—my tupelos and tamaracks,
my amethyst and tourmaline, my chickadees and peepers.

these are the children i did not create—
neither mother nor father
to sister or brother.

i give them a world not mine to give,
nor theirs to call their own—
but a step-gift, a step-life to cherish and savor.

i did not create this love, it's true
but my step-girl, my step-boy,
this step-love's for you.

One Good Turn

I was driving with my grandson.
He was hitting me with his juice box.
I told him about the golden rule
and he stopped.

Later, as I said goodbye,
I kissed the back of his head.
He was already eating an apple
and didn't look up.

As I walked to my car,
he came to the door,
called me back
and said,

Pa, remember the golden rule?
and kissed
the back of my head.

Tethered

The other day, our grandbaby Skipper
held on to her brother Mack, uncertain
of anyone less familiar, held on

like a weasel to her prey,
her teeth sunk into his shoulder,
reminiscent of a burdock seed on a sock

or a limpet on a rock—how
desperately I hold on
to what I'm already held by—tethered

like wave to water, sand grain to
beach, breath to air, held
by arms I can never

fall out of, and still, I cling
to the cliff, as if the ground
weren't what my feet are made of.

What Words Miss

I have never been one to inscribe a line longer than
necessary. The less said the better. Words come and go.
Even saints think in language, while what they think about can
best inhere to themselves. Saint Francis, who would never know
Claire the way he thought of her, took snow for a loving wife
instead, took to laying in mountain drifts as in her bed
and fought with all the little Claires who occupied his head.
Silence, at least, might be a refuge, a doorway to life
intrinsically less tripped by words, more likely to instill us
with faith in what words miss, a living that lives to fill us.

Things to Think

after Robert Bly

Think the way you thought
before you were born,
when you were rain or stone,
how you longed to be human
and promised yourself that
this time, it would be different—
how you wouldn't snore,
or if you did, it would put
everyone who heard it to sleep—
and you might get fat
from potato chips, but each one
you consumed would take
a little pain from the world.

Think the next time your doorbell rings
you've gotten a package from Jupiter—
the saffron glow of its planet-sized heart—
think of being that generous.

The next time you see a shopping cart,
think that it carries your unborn child,
the career you left behind,
the power to stop a war—
and you have to choose just one.

Think when you mail a letter,
that you've sent your fear of death
to someone who finds it hilarious,
whose laughter turns to falling stars
that, one by one, can bring
the world to silence.

We Didn't Think of Death

We didn't think of death when we first met.
Our bodies felt each other out for truth.
The suns that never lighted us had set—
the brighter day we hoped for in our youth.
Yet there you were, a truth at last revealed:
A grace, a gift, a molten light, a sun.
We found in love how broken could be healed,
how fetters on the spirit come undone.
Though marriage long and deep has been a jewel,
opening our eyes to every facet,
the truth is life itself, in death, is cruel,
void of any way to leave or pass it.
In loving you, I've learned to love this life,
worth dying for, as long as you're my wife.

When I say I fell in love

I don't mean tripped and skinned my knee,
or even like a flowerpot from an upstairs window,
I mean rocket ship to Venus, free-falling to the moon,
all we have is what the fruit feels between losing the branch
and landing on the Earth, holding onto each other,
never let it end, it just feels so good falling, in love, with you.

Anniversary

I would grow blackberries for you, my love,
as long as soil bears sweetness, and air
the burgeoning bulbous berries, the sun
a willing captive of the royal purple juice.
I would be the roots immoveable, the vines reaching
for more and more of a life with you, something
your mouth dreams of, something your hand tenders.
I would be the berries in your garden;
the thornless branch that nevertheless
can make us bleed; the unripe, the ripened,
the overripe berries in your deep-stained hands;
the seeds between your teeth for your tongue to worry.
Yes, I would grow blackberries for you longer still,
in that garden where vine and vintner, berry and maker
dwell together, and even there, my love,
would I bow and proffer that black bowl of ever
for your joy.

The Wave

The Museum of Science has an exhibit about waves,
a long, clear box, with a paddle at one end,
pushing the water as a whale tail might,
though inexhaustible and relentless
as a tumor.

After my granddaughter's MRI, I watch as kids, with implicit faith,
run their hands down the sides of the case, convinced
they are making the waves move.
There is sand at the end
of the box,

and everyone can see how, one by one, the waves lose more
and more of themselves, as the angle of the sand grows
steeper. I remember my relief, after the doctor who,
like me, sometimes sits on her hands, showed us
her results—

the small folds of the brain, the clear,
bright image, inexhaustibly wavy
itself—and asked again,
if we had any
questions.

There Is Nothing but Space Between Us

A cosmic swirl of dust and need,
all the little densities—
the moons and worlds,
spoons and rocks, the gnats
and rain and trains and trees—
all the stuff that matter makes
is mostly filled with nothing.

And the nothing that is mostly there
is held in the bigger nothing,
and the presence of this nothing-space
is the something that we live in.

In the story that I tell myself,
we see each other as space—
so space holds space when space
needs holding.

Inis Mor

I wandered up a stony track
And found myself among the green
And sat beside a shining leaf
And there I laid my offering.

There I sat and there she rooted
Rain clouds grew and we grew closer
Felt together what atoms feel
What drew the rain down to the soil
And wind into the feather.

Now I'm inside the cottage warm
And she's inside the evening rain
And strange to love the ones we love
The way that nature joins us.

For this I left a copper coin
On the stony ledge beside her—
That there be days the sun might track
More brightly on those leaves
And remind her.

Tashlik

A Hebrew word meaning "to cast away," tashlik is the name of a ritual of repentance performed at the Jewish High Holiday Yom Kippur.

Go to the river.
If not the river—the pond, the sea
if not the sea—the sink, the gutter;
if none of these, cry into your hand;
if your eyes are dry, spit.

Reach into the pockets
where you keep small change,
keys, sweets, the lint of days
and anything else that needs
clearing out—hate, guilt.

If you have no pockets,
reach in the dirt
and pick up a stone.

Let tar, sap, sludge
leak out, the vile, the craven
sink into this stone
and cast it all away.

Unlikely stone,
as you fall from me
turn into bread,
to apples and honey.

Let me begin again.

About the Author

Chuck Madansky finds solace and inspiration living by a pond on Cape Cod in Massachusetts. A former virologist and currently semi-retired as a psychotherapist, Chuck received the 2010 Cornerstone Award of the Barnstable County Human Rights Commission for his efforts to raise awareness of and bring an end to US torture. His poetry has been published in *Passager, Pure Slush, Muddy River Poetry Review,* and the *Cape Cod Poetry Review* and has been featured as part of Poetry Sunday, a production of Cape Cod's NPR station. The grandfather of 6, Chuck, lives with his wife, the poet and playwright Wilderness Sarchild, and their beloved dog Ruby.

www.ingramcontent.com/pod-product-compliance
Lightning Source LLC
Chambersburg PA
CBHW020730100426
42735CB00038B/1454